THE HELIOTROPE BOUQUET BY SCOTT JOPLIN & LOUIS CHAUVIN

by Eric Overmyer

Based on a libretto by Eric Overmyer from an idea by Roger Trefousse

357 W 20th St., NY NY 10011
212 627-1055

THE HELIOTROPE BOUQUET BY SCOTT JOPLIN &
LOUIS CHAUVIN © Copyright 1993 by Eric Overmyer

First printing: June 1993
ISBN: 0-88145-108-8

Book design: Marie Donovan
Word processing: Microsoft Word for Windows
Typographic controls: Xerox Ventura Publisher 2.0 PE
Typeface: Palatino
Printed on recycled acid-free paper and bound in the
USA.

BY ERIC OVERMYER
PUBLISHED BY BROADWAY PLAY
PUBLISHING

NATIVE SPEECH (1984)
ON THE VERGE (1986)
IN PERPETUITY
THROUGHOUT THE UNIVERSE (1989)
IN A PIG'S VALISE (1989)
MI VIDA LOCA (1991)
DON QUIXOTE DE LA JOLLA (1993)
DARK RAPTURE (1993)

ABOUT THE AUTHOR

Eric Overmyer is the recipient of grants and fellowships from the McKnight Foundation, the Le Comte Du Nouy Foundation, the New York Foundation for the Arts, the Rockefeller Foundation, and the NEA. He was an Associate Artist at Center Stage, Baltimore from 1984 to 1991, a Visiting Professor of Playwriting at Yale School of Drama, and an Associate Artist at the Yale Rep, 1991-2, and Mentor for the Mark Taper Playwriting Workshop, 1992. He has also taught playwriting at the Playwrights Horizons/NYU School.

ON THE VERGE has been performed extensively throughout the United States, Canada, Australia, and the UK, and has been translated into French and Norwegian, and performed in those languages in Paris and Oslo. IN PERPETUITY THROUGHOUT THE UNIVERSE has been translated into Quebecois by the prominent Quebecois playwright, Rene-Daniel DuBois, and performed in Montreal.

This play is dedicated to Stan Wojewodski, Jr

ORIGINAL PRODUCTION

THE HELIOTROPE BOUQUET BY SCOTT JOPLIN
AND LOUIS CHAUVIN was originally produced by
Center Stage, Baltimore, Maryland (Stan Wojewodski,
Jr, Artistic Director; Peter Culman, Managing Director).
The first performance was on 15 Feb 1991 with the
following cast and creative contributors:

JOPLIN .... Monti Sharp
SPANISH MARY/LOTTIE/BELLE ....Essene R
HANNAH .... Linda Cavell
SPICE .... Ellen Bethea
JOY .... Gina Torres
FELICITY ....Denise Diggs
TRICK JOHN/DISAPPEARING SAM .... Dion Graham
TURPIN .... Jeffrey V Thompson
KEELER .... L Peter Callender
CHAUVIN ....Victor Mack
STARK .... Wil Love

Director .... Stan Wojewodski, Jr
Set design .... Christopher Barreca
Costume design ....Catherine Zuber
Lighting design ....Richard Pilbrow
Sound design ....Janet Kalas
Music director .... Dwight Andrews
Choreographer ....Donald Byrd
Dramaturgs .... Mona Heinze, James Magruder
Recorded pianist ....William Ransom
Stage management   Julie Thompson, James Mountcastle

THE HELIOTROPE BOUQUET BY SCOTT JOPLIN
AND LOUIS CHAUVIN was subsequently produced
by the La Jolla Playhouse (Des McAnuff, Artistic
Director; Alan Levey, Managing Director) with the
following cast changes:

JOPLIN . . . . John Cothran, Jr
LOTTIE/BELLE . . . . Judy Ann Elder
JOY . . . . June Jones
TURPIN . . . . Keith Smith
KEELER . . . . SaMi Chester

Both productions were in association with AT&T
OnStage.

Playwrights Horizons, Inc., New York City, produced
THE HELIOTROPE BOUQUET BY SCOTT JOPLIN
AND LOUIS CHAUVIN Off-Broadway in 1993.

The play takes place in a Harlem rooming house, Christmas Eve, 1916, where Scott Joplin lives with his second wife, Lottie; in Dream New Orleans, c. 1900, in a sporting house called The House of Blue Light; in the Rosebud Cafe, St. Louis, 1905; and in Chicago, 1906, in an opium den known as The Sportin' Life.

The play should be performed without intermission.

Characters

JOPLIN
SPANISH MARY/LOTTIE/BELLE
HANNAH
SPICE
JOY
FELICITY
TRICK JOHN/DISAPPEARING SAM
TURPIN
KEELER
CHAUVIN
STARK

Part One

(JOPLIN's Dream)

(Dream New Orleans. A sporting house called The House of Blue Light.)

(A man is sleeping, lying across a piano. This is JOPLIN. On top of the piano is an electric Christmas tree.)

(It is just before dawn. August. The light is soft and beautiful.)

(The women of the House enter: JOY, FELICITY, SPICE, SPANISH MARY, and HANNAH.)

                                    JOY
Just before dawn.

                          SPANISH MARY
(West Indian accent) Cool yet.

                               HANNAH
Before the day turns to fire.

(The air is filled with flashes of colored light, shooting stars.)

                                    JOY
Look! Shooting stars!

(The women ooo and la.)

                                  SPICE
Lord. Shooting stars.

FELICITY
Oh, the air is full of colored light.

JOY
Nobody knows shooting stars, what they are.

SPICE
They say the Earth is passing through the memory of an
ancient world.

SPANISH MARY
Atlantis. Everybody knows that would be Atlantis.

WOMEN
(Echoing) Atlantis.

SPICE
Was drowned.

SPANISH MARY
Was not drowned, was hurled into darkness.

JOY
That was Pompeii.

HANNAH
Pompeii the irredeemable.

SPANISH MARY
Atlantis. Hurled into darkness.

(The shooting stars vanish. The dark lightens. Dawn.)

FELICITY
They're gone.

JOY
Melted by the sun.

HANNAH

Scared away by foolish talk.

SPICE

Like snow. Melted like snow.

SPANISH MARY

You never seen snow.

SPICE

I heard. I heard about snow.

FELICITY

Lord, it's cool now.

JOY

For a moment.

SPANISH MARY

There's a lacy breeze.

HANNAH

Lacy breeze fluttering.

SPICE

Lacy breeze.

JOY

Spanish moss lacy in the live oak trees.

FELICITY

Fluttering.

JOY

Morning, morning, morning.

FELICITY

Morning in The House of Blue Light.

(Sound of water, flowing over stone.)

(The women wash themselves, pouring water from pitchers into small porcelain basins. For a moment just the sound of water, and dipping hands. Then a customer, TRICK JOHN, stumbles in, piercing the perfect stillness.)

TRICK JOHN

Sportin' house, take my money, make me sick.
My head feels like a thunderstorm, hot 'n sore.
Full of heat lightning, cracklin' from cloud to cloud.
My eyes are plump as two parboiled peaches.
My tongue's swoll up like it walked halfway to
Egypt on its hands and feet.

(The women laugh.)

HANNAH

What's the matter with you, Trick John, you should
have been long gone—

WOMEN
(Echoing one another) Long gone, long gone—

HANNAH

Long gone by now.

TRICK JOHN

Had a dream I couldn't crawl out of. Dreamed I went to
my own funeral. Dreamed I looked down and there I
was, laid out in a black suit and silk top hat, solid silver
pocket watch tickin' away in my vest pocket, twenty-
dollar gold pieces on my eyes. And all the women were
weeping.

(The women laugh.)

WOMEN
(Echoing) Over you? My, my. Not you.

TRICK JOHN

Over me, yes yes, over me. Weeping and wailing,
talking about what a sweet man I was. Just put that on
my tombstone: He was a sweet man. That's why they
called him Sugarcane.

WOMEN

(Laughing) Sugarcane.

FELICITY

They don't call you Sugarcane, they call you Trick John.

(FELICITY *goes to* TRICK JOHN, *wraps herself around him.*)

TRICK JOHN

Don't you put your smell on me.

FELICITY

I've licked your eyes. I've stained your blood.
You'll never wash my smell away. Sugarcane.

(She kisses him deeply. He sighs.)

TRICK JOHN

Oh, yes. Oh, my. Oh, God. Goodbye, baby, goodbye.

SPANISH MARY

Bye bye, now.

(TRICK JOHN *stumbles out. The women laugh.*)

WOMEN

(Echoing) Bye bye, now. Bye bye.

HANNAH

Morning. Morning, morning, morning.

JOY

Colors of the morning in The House of Blue Light.

SPICE
Magnolia breeze—

FELICITY
Ivory with a purple bruise, like the inside of my thigh—

HANNAH
Cotton taste in my mouth like old smoke swirling—

JOY
Tastes smokey red like whiskey, white like cigars—

SPICE
Sunlight piercing through a broken shutter slat—

SPANISH MARY
Dust sparks dancing in the tired air—

FELICITY
Silk chemise draped over the back of an ebony chair—

HANNAH
Cypress mist rising soft off the river—

JOY
Dew drop dripping down a sweet banana leaf—

FELICITY
Bowl of strawberries covered in cream—

SPICE
Handful of rhinestone rubies scattered across a
blood-stained oriental rug—

HANNAH
Half a glass of bourbon under the bed—

FELICITY
Dollars dancing in the front parlor—

HANNAH

Sweet shuffle of money rubbing up against itself—

FELICITY

Money making money—

SPANISH MARY

Counting the money, money and love—

JOY

Damp sheets—

HANNAH

Musky shutters—

SPANISH MARY

Chasing the musk outdoors after a long night—

HANNAH

After a long night—

JOY

After a long night—

FELICITY

After a long night—

SPANISH MARY

After the blue ballet of money and love—

WOMEN

(*Echoing*) All night, all night long—

SPICE

Blue light shining—

HANNAH

Cool, cool morning—

JOY
I feel so sweet, just to touch myself—

HANNAH
Be by myself—

SPICE
I feel so sweet—

FELICITY
So sweet—

JOY
Time for sleep. Sleep the day away.

WOMEN
(Echoing) Sleep the day, sleep the day away.

(The women stretch and sigh. JOPLIN wakes with a start. The light changes. Harlem, New York, 1916. Rundown rooming house. The women vanish, except for SPANISH MARY, who throws on a robe, and becomes JOPLIN's wife, LOTTIE. JOPLIN painfully unclenches his hands.)

JOPLIN
Do my hands please, Lottie. Do my hands.

(LOTTIE sighs, goes to him, takes his outstretched hand, kneads.)

LOTTIE
Bad dreams, Joplin.

JOPLIN
Strange. I had strange dreams. All kind of strange and wonderful. New Orleans. The House of Blue Light.

LOTTIE
Oh, Joplin.

JOPLIN

You were there. Upstairs. With Trick John. No account,
ne'er-do-well.

LOTTIE

That's enough.

JOPLIN

Dream every night of The House of Blue Light.
This is what comes of keeping whores.

LOTTIE

And how are we to live, tell me that. Ragtime's over,
ragtime's gone, ragtime's done.

JOPLIN

Six horses.

LOTTIE

Horses?

JOPLIN

In my dream. Six horses. Stamping in the black surf.
Paper-white hides, and moon-colored manes. Black
water, black as coffee, and clear as a box of heaven. The
water thick and hot as blood, and the surf burns them,
burns and roils, foams white and surges up under their
bellies, scalds their eyes. White-paper hides, and eyes
as big and pale and luminous as little moons. *(Beat)* The
deep draws them. The moon draws them. Lays down
a sparkle on the water. They follow that sparkle, like
children follow a stranger who's got sweets and money.
The sea calls them. Calls us. Always. We have a longing
for it. *(Beat)* Then they drown. They choke, and they
drown. Nostrils streaming black blood. The water will
not let them go. And as the horses drown they have a
memory of sunlight, and a longing for it, and for fields,
and tall grass. A longing for dust in their mouths. For

simple sweet rain instead of salty surf, and for sugar
sky. Sugar sky. But they cannot catch their breath. The
water will not give them up. They drown. The sea calls
them, and they drown. They burn and they drown,
longing for sunlight. Moon-colored hooves, and white,
white eyes.

(He stops. Recollects himself. Turns to LOTTIE.*)*

JOPLIN
This was my dream. Six white horses drowning,
burning and drowning in the coffee-colored surf.
And then the horses disappeared, and we came to the
sportin' house. The House of Blue Light. You were
there, but you weren't you, you were Spanish Mary.

LOTTIE
Hush, now, that's enough. Spanish Mary. That's
enough. It's the sickness on you. The fever on you,
God help us.

JOPLIN
Comes of keeping whores. That's why I dream of
The House of Blue Light, every night.

LOTTIE
How else are we to live? My God. Besides, this is not
a sportin' house. We just let rooms. Whores got to live
somewhere, too.

JOPLIN
I am taken away from myself.

LOTTIE
I'll bring you coffee.

JOPLIN
Black as fever, please. And hot white milk with foam.
Chicory. That little lick of New Orleans. And beignets.

Dusty white with sugar. I need sweetness. I crave it.
Sweetness in my mouth. Shoo the taste of that vile
dream away.

LOTTIE

I'll bring plums, too.

JOPLIN

Glossy black and purple.

LOTTIE

Sweet and cold.

(LOTTIE *goes.* JOPLIN *moves to the piano.*)

JOPLIN

Sweet and cold. Man needs sweetness. Sweetness
belongs in a man's mouth. Man should always have
sweetness in his mouth.

(*He opens the bench, and brings forth a large manscript,
the* Treemonisha *score.*)

JOPLIN

Still time. Still time. While there's still time.

(*He sits at the piano. He hits a note. He writes. He hits
another note. He writes. Another. He writes. Another.
Listens to the note fade away. He puts the manuscript down.
Gazes in silence a moment. Then a dream of ragtime phrase
plays, echoing in the ether. He listens, lost in reverie.*)

JOPLIN

A dream of ragtime phrase. Oh I was young and easy
when I wrote that. Young and dumb. Thoughtless.
Thought I'd live forever. Play forever. Have strong
hands forever. And the music would come. Just come,
and come, and come. Like a woman. In waves. Come
like a woman. Come upon me like heat, and come

through me like lightning. Music like heat lightning
rolling across a sultry St. Louis summer afternoon.

(A burst of music. The lights change.)

(St. Louis. The Rosebud Cafe. 1905.)

*(*TURPIN, *the proprietor, enters, trailed by the other piano
professors,* DISAPPEARING SAM *and* KEELER, *and* SPICE,
JOY, FELICITY, *and* HANNAH.*)*

TURPIN
Cutting contest. Cutting contest. Make a mark, find a
line. Tell your business. Call on God and see if He's at
home. See if He's at home to you tonight.

FELICITY
And who are you when you're at home, Mr. Turpin?

TURPIN
This is my place. This bucket of blood is my home.
So I guess you could say I'm God. At least hereabouts.

FELICITY
I could say that. But that don't make it true.

TURPIN
If I ain't God, I'll have to do until the real thing comes
along.

*(*TURPIN *gestures to the electric Christmas tree on the piano.)*

TURPIN
Voila! Let there be light.

(The tree lights up. Cheers from the crowd.)

TURPIN
Told you. Told you I was God in this house.

JOPLIN

Wait, wait, you're confused. July ain't Christmas.

TURPIN

No, it ain't. But it ain't July, Joplin, it's Christmas time
at the Rosebud Cafe, St. Louis Missouri, Nineteen
Aught Five.

JOPLIN

Hot as Hades outside.

TURPIN

It's gonna snow like an orphan tonight. You're burning
up, my friend. Sweating like a sick pig. Been messing
with them poxy gals.

JOPLIN

No, I never.

(The women laugh.)

FELICITY

Never touched them.

JOY

Never loved them.

HANNAH

Never came around.

JOPLIN

No, I never.

HANNAH

Could have sworn that was you.

SPICE

Could have sworn that was your sweet body inside
mine.

JOPLIN
I'm a married man. Got a baby girl. Don't hold with the sportin' life, never have.

(BELLE *appears.*)

BELLE
Joplin?

JOPLIN
Belle.

SPICE
Could have sworn that was you.

HANNAH
Could have sworn that was your sweet body inside mine.

FELICITY
I remember you.

JOPLIN
No.

FELICITY
Joplin, sure.

SPICE
Young piano professor.

JOY
Come upstairs, young piano professor.

JOPLIN
That was long ago. I was young.

FELICITY
You're still young. Come upstairs.

JOPLIN

No. Don't entice me.

(The women laugh.)

WOMEN

(Echoing) Entice me.

(JOPLIN *goes to* BELLE. *They kiss.)*

TURPIN

Come on, come on. Now, let there be music! Cutting contest.

DISAPPEARING SAM

That right, cutting contest. Who the best?

KEELER

Cutting contest. Call on God, and see if He's at home. See if He's at home to you tonight.

DISAPPEARING SAM

Home to me, I'm the one.

(TURPIN *brandishes a big gold medal.)*

TURPIN

I got a solid gold medal for the premier professor, for the finest purveyor of pianistic legerdemain. Solid gold, and nothing but.

JOY

Is it genuine?

TURPIN

You tell me.

(He displays medal, hands it to JOY, *who bites on it, considers.)*

JOY

Tastes genuine.

(She hands it back to TURPIN.*)*

TURPIN

Tastes genuine, is genuine. Solid gold, and nothing but.
Joplin, you go first.

JOPLIN

No, I can't. I wasn't there. I just heard about it later.

TURPIN

That's right. You were somewhere else that night.
Somewheres else. Prob'ly with some poxy gal. 'Scuse
me. I forgot. You don't hold with the sportin' life.

JOPLIN

Never have. I'm a married man. Got a baby girl. Belle—

(He looks around for BELLE, *who has disappeared. The
women laugh.* TURPIN *points to* DISAPPEARING SAM.*)*

TURPIN

Disappearing Sam, you're on.

HANNAH

Let me hear angels.

SPICE

Rapture me honey.

JOY

Send me to heaven.

FELICITY

Send me to hell.

(The women laugh. DISAPPEARING SAM *gestures to the
piano. As he speaks, music plays. The women ooo and la.)*

DISAPPEARING SAM

They call me Disappearing Sam because I am forever on
the lam. Quicker than true love, slyer than a cobweb.
My feet so fast they keep this dusty old world spinning
'round. I'm here, I'm there, and then I'm gone, darker
than midnight and deeper than the dawn.

FELICITY

Disappearing Sam, uh, huh,—you know where the
treasure's kept—Oh goodness, darling, Disappearing,
stroke those ivory keys, please.

DISAPPEARING SAM

Don't blink or you might miss me. Don't think that you
can kiss me, any more than you can kiss your shadow's
shadow. I'm a whirling dervish, a handful of
quicksilver, a scrap of birdsong gone fluttering by.
A moonbeam. A zephyr. And when I die, when I'm
dead and gone, you'll feel this old world start to slow
on down. Midnight won't ever be so deep, the dawn
won't ring so rosy bright, and nothing will ever taste
quite so sweet again.

(Music finishes playing. The women applaud.)

FELICITY

Darling Disappearing, don't you go disappearin' yet.

(She kisses him passionately.)

DISAPPEARING SAM

Perhaps I'll stick around.

HANNAH

Wasn't that sweet?

WOMEN

(Echoing) So sweet.

FELICITY

Wasn't that succulent?

WOMEN

(Echoing) Mmmm, succulent.

TURPIN

Sweet, maybe—but not succulent.

WOMEN

(Echoing) You're wrong, you're wrong, oh, you're so
wrong.

DISAPPEARING SAM

You never heard playing like that before.

WOMEN

(Echoing) That's right, that's right, that's right.

TURPIN

Just every day of my life. My sweet old mother plays
better 'n that, and she got the shakes.

DISAPPEARING SAM

And you'll be a lucky man, you ever do again.

HANNAH

Too true.

WOMEN

(Echoing) Too true, too true.

TURPIN

I'll take my chances. Keeler, you're on.

(KEELER *steps forward.*)

KEELER

Now I know why they call you Disappearing Sam.
Your playing was so tender, so delicate, so truly

heartfelt—I almost fell asleep. I almost drifted off
to the land of dreamy dreams. A lovely lullaby of
hummingbirds and lilac bushes. A touch of dewdrop
and a minty lip. *(Winks)* But I got something saltier for
you, Ladies.

HANNAH
Ooh, I like salty.

KEELER
A diversion of my own devising. A concoction.
A fascination. A ramdoozle. A fandango, and a
slow tango.

FELICITY
Do tell, Keeler. Show us your two-hand magic.

JOY
Let us get a grip on what you do.

KEELER
Ladies and gentlemen. A confectionary delectation for
the whole collected lacadation. For the entire assembled
aggravation. Calculated to captivate. Guaranteed to
give your very marrow a thrill.

TURPIN
Perhaps I should give you the gold medal for talking,
just for talking.

KEELER
Stand aside. Prepare to be moved. Prepare to be
raptured. Prepare to taste ambrosia on the lips of
angels. Prepare to swoon from the sheer celestial
vibrations of Saturn's rainbow rings. Y'all better
find a soft place to land.

(The men and women ooo, hoot, ahhh, and holler.
KEELER *tips his brim, acknowledging the accolades.)*

KEELER

Yeah, you're right.

(KEELER *gestures to the piano; music plays.*)

DISAPPEARING SAM

Don't you hurt nobody, now.

KEELER

I got something that will make plain women pretty, and
pretty women forever young. Take the ache from the
back of a workin' man. Make vinegar taste like wine.
Make raindrops shine like diamonds. Make a bee sting
feel like a kiss, and bring tears to the boss's eyes. Turn
cornbread into cobbler, and cobbler into Thanksgiving
Day.

JOY

God, the man can play.

FELICITY

I'm stirred, I melt.

SPICE

Me, too.

KEELER

I don't have to talk. My playing talks sweeter than
any man's melodies. Heavenly elixir. Sheer nectar.
Pandemonium. I put my hands on a lonely out-of-tune
rickety on-its-last-legs honkey-tonk piana and make it
sound like an entire high-class top hat 'n tails sympathy
orchestra. So listen, listen, listen.

WOMEN

(Echoing) Oooo.

HANNAH

Now that I've heard heaven, stab me with dull scissors,
and I'll die slow, but happy.

*(Music finishes playing with a flourish. Applause from the
entire "lacadation"—except* TURPIN.*)*

TURPIN

I was not taken off to heaven. I was not transported to
distant shores. I did not hear no angels in the hallway.

FELICITY

That's because you're an insensitive man.

JOY

A brute.

HANNAH

A bully.

SPICE

And you cheat at cards.

TURPIN

I do the best I can.

DISAPPEARING SAM

You made up your mind beforehand, quit wastin' time,
tell us who the winner is and let's go get drunk.

TURPIN

I don't know who the winner is, but I do know who the
winners ain't.

KEELER

Do the best you can. I dare you. Won't be good enough.
Not near good enough.

*(*TURPIN *moves to the piano.)*

TURPIN

Talking won't get it.

WOMEN

(Echoing) That's right, never does. Talking won't get it.

TURPIN

Talking won't get it, but playing will. Clear the cotton from out your ears and listen up.

(TURPIN gestures to the piano. Then he talks as the music plays.)

TURPIN

A dream of ragtime rapture. Just a phrase. A taste.
A lick. A breath. A breeze. A dream of ragtime rapture.
Something to stir your heart and remind you of your
life's best days, of the sweet moments, all the sweet
moments, strung together like a handful of colored
glass, and you can see down through 'em, each and
every one, to the very last time you tasted wine, or stole
a kiss, or felt the sun shine and the breeze blow, and
thought some days, this ain't so bad, this life.

(The women prefer him clearly.)

HANNAH

Oh, Turpin's got the touch.

JOY

I swan, make my head spin.

SPICE

Make my backbone rock and bend.

FELICITY

Oh, my.

JOY

Hot and sweet.

HANNAH

Sweet and cruel.

FELICITY

As homemade sin.

JOY

Now here's a man, I swan.

(The music finishes.)

TURPIN

Well, Keeler, it's clear, the ladies have their say.
By popular acclaim, I give the medal to myself.

DISAPPEARING SAM

Cheat. Fixer. Con man. Dirty Dog. *(Howls)* Ah oooo!

KEELER

They work for you, the poxy bitches. Who do you think
you're fooling, who? Fool. You're not fit to play the
parlor of the skeeziest, most scrofulous cathouse in
town.

TURPIN

I scoff at your playing, Keeler. I cut you bad.

KEELER

Then scoff at this.

(KEELER draws a pistol.)

TURPIN

Lunatic.

KEELER

I pity you, fool.

*(TURPIN draws a pistol. They fire at one another.
The ladies scream.)*

(KEELER falls, and TURPIN runs out. Everyone leaves. A silent moment. A voice comes out of the shadows.)

CHAUVIN
Wasn't that way at all.

(CHAUVIN steps out of the shadows, where he's been watching, and approaches JOPLIN.)

JOPLIN
No.

CHAUVIN
You remembered it all wrong.

JOPLIN
Yes.

CHAUVIN
And you forgot me.

JOPLIN
Yes. No. I've never forgotten you.

CHAUVIN
Everyone's forgotten me.

JOPLIN
Not me. Not Joplin. I remember you every day of my life. Louis Chauvin.

CHAUVIN
Keeler died.

JOPLIN
That's right.

CHAUVIN
Turpin went to jail.

JOPLIN

That's right.

CHAUVIN

But that was later. And it wasn't about a cutting contest.

JOPLIN

No.

CHAUVIN

It was over a woman.

(JOPLIN *turns to see* BELLE *standing on the edge of the light.*)

JOPLIN

Belle.

CHAUVIN

No, not Belle.

JOPLIN

My wife, Belle.

CHAUVIN

No, not Belle I said.

(She disappears.)

CHAUVIN

Some other, some poxy whore, some clapped-up bitch.

JOPLIN

The sportin' life. I warned you.

(He looks back at BELLE. *She's gone.)*

CHAUVIN

All I knew, the sportin' life. Playing the parlor. Money
and spunk. All kinds of spending going on upstairs.
And look at you, Joplin. Nerves rotting away. Brain
turning to gravy.

JOPLIN

Sins of my youth.

CHAUVIN

Lot of good it ever did you.

JOPLIN

What?

CHAUVIN

Worrying. Always worrying. One eye on tomorrow.
Mr. Cautious Joplin. I won that contest.

JOPLIN

I remember.

(Music. They all come back—KEELER, TURPIN,
DISAPPEARING SAM, *and the women, except* BELLE.
CHAUVIN *steps back out of the light. As before:* JOPLIN's
memory, revised.)

TURPIN

Cutting contest. Cutting contest.

DISAPPEARING SAM

That right. Who the best?

KEELER

Call on God and see if He's at home. See if He's at home
to you tonight.

DISAPPEARING SAM

Home to me. I'm the one. A zephyr. A moonbeam.
A scrap of birdsong gone fluttering by—

KEELER

A concoction, a delectation, a flash of fascination for the
entire assembled aggravation, for the whole collected
lacadation.

TURPIN

A handful of colored glass, remind you of your life's best moments, ain't so bad—

DISAPPEARING SAM

So listen—

KEELER

Listen—

TURPIN

Listen—

(The ladies prefer TURPIN *again.)*

HANNAH

Oh Turpin's got the touch.

JOY

I swan, make my head spin.

SPICE

Make my backbone rock and bend.

FELICITY

Oh, my.

JOY

Hot and sweet.

HANNAH

Sweet and cruel.

FELICITY

As homemade sin.

JOY

Now here's a man, I swan.

(The music finishes. TURPIN *beams.)*

TURPIN

It's clear, the ladies have their say. By popular acclaim I
give the medal to myself.

DISAPPEARING SAM

Cheat. Fixer. Con man. *(Howls)* Ah ooooooooooooooo.
Dirty Dog.

KEELER

They work for you, the poxy bitches. Who do you think
you're foolin', who?

TURPIN

I cut you all bad.

(CHAUVIN steps out of the shadows.)

CHAUVIN

You ain't cut me.

TURPIN

Louis Chauvin.

(The crowd murmurs his name.)

TURPIN

The legendary Louis Chauvin. Where you been?

CHAUVIN

Waiting my turn.

TURPIN

We been saving it. It's your turn now. Take your turn.
Do your best.

*(CHAUVIN nods, gestures at piano; music plays.
The crowd is transfixed.)*

CHAUVIN

White moon drifting in a deep blue sky
Full moon
Afternoon sky
What do they call that daytime moon
I wonder
God's one good eye
Maybe
Waking when it's dark
Playing piano till just before dawn
After it's all done
After it's all done
Juke joint gin mill honky tonk gut bucket tango palace
Sawdust and smoke
Coffee with a shot of rye
A woman slipping out of her dress
The back of her neck
All cool and sweet
Cold cold water on a sultry summer day
Deep sleep and no dreams
A ticket on the next train out of town
And enough money to get me
From here
To there.

(He finishes. A moment of silence, then cheers and applause.
TURPIN *hangs a gold medal around* CHAUVIN's *neck.)*

TURPIN

The winner, and always champion. As long as memory
serves—Louis Chauvin.

(Cheers and applause)

JOPLIN

You were the piano wizard. You won the fair, too.

DISAPPEARING SAM

The World's Fair.

KEELER

The Great Exposition of Nineteen Aught Four. The
World's Greatest Cutting Contest. The World's Premier
Piano Professors. From the Four Corners of the Globe,
from France and Abyssinia—

ALL

(Echoing) France and Abyssinia—

KEELER

Connoisseurs of the Keyboards, from as far away as
Budapest and Madagascar—

ALL

(Echoing) Talking about Budapest and Madagascar—

KEELER

Step up, step up, step up, step right up—

CHAUVIN

And be amazed.

(CHAUVIN *steps forward.*)

CHAUVIN

This is where I'm s'posed to brag. S'posed to tell you
how brilliant like lightning flash in a bottle I am. How
slick, how wicked positively, how mellifluous, how sly,
how absolutely splendid a man I am. And I am. It's
true. But why brag?

HANNAH

He is, it's true.

SPICE

Sweet and flash—

JOY

Brilliant and slick—

FELICITY

Mellifluous and salty.

HANNAH

No brag, no brag, just fact.

SPICE

Louis Chauvin. Funny-looking man. Look like a frog
fell in a liquor barrel. But he could squeeze my heart
like no man could.

HANNAH

I could hear him in my room, playing those rags. He'd
take my mind off what I was doing, take me away from
myself.

FELICITY

He could make me enjoy it, even enjoy it.

WOMEN

(Echoing) Enjoy it? You?

JOY

Not you.

FELICITY

It's true, even me.

JOY

Must have been in league with the Devil then.

WOMEN

(Echoing) Must have been.

(The women laugh.)

CHAUVIN

This is where I'm s'posed to tell you how I came to be
a natural genius. Untaught and unschooled, a child of

nature. A primitive artiste. An idiot savant. Music in
my breath and God in my fingertips. This is where I'm
s'posed to say I'm the seventh son of a seventh son.
Talk about mojo.

MEN

(Echoing) Mojo—

CHAUVIN

And hoodoo—

MEN

(Echoing) Hoodoo—

CHAUVIN

And Saint John the Conqueroo.

ALL

(Echoing) Sweet Saint John the Conqueroo.

CHAUVIN

How a black cat scared my mama, when I was in her
belly. How she took me to a gypsy woman when I was
born.

HANNAH

And what did that gypsy woman say?

CHAUVIN

All kind of strange and wonderful.

WOMEN

(Echoing) Strange and wonderful.

CHAUVIN

All kind of strange and wonderful.

WOMEN

(Echoing) Strange and wonderful.

JOY

Is it true?

HANNAH

Is it true?

FELICITY

Is it true?

CHAUVIN

Is what true?

JOY

The black cat and the seventh son of a seventh son, and
what the gypsy woman say.

FELICITY

Is it true?

HANNAH

Is it true?

SPICE

Is it true?

JOY

Is it true?

CHAUVIN

No, it ain't true. Just foolish talk. That's all.

JOPLIN

But it is true you could hear a song and play it back
note for note. Just hear it once, and play it perfect.
I know that's true. I saw you do that. More than once.

CHAUVIN

God blessed me, that's what's true. Not the Devil. God
gave me an ear and a way to think in notes of music,

like bits of colored glass. Like water flowing. Rings
falling. Something dropping. Something hitting
something else. That's what sound is. Keys on strings.
Dropping like rain. Water on stone. *(Pause)* It's a gift
and cannot be explained, but that don't mean it's magic.
Ain't magic.

KEELER
You played like magic. You cut us all. Then you went
away. Disappeared.

CHAUVIN
Chicago.

ALL
(Echoing) That's right, Chicago.

TURPIN
Heard you did the same thing there.

CHAUVIN
What'd you hear?

TURPIN
Heard you put everyone to shame.

CHAUVIN
Heard that, did you?

TURPIN
Yes, I did.

ALL
(Echoing) That's right, that's right, Chicago, put
everyone to shame.

CHAUVIN
Well, you heard wrong. *(Beat)* I didn't do nothin' in
Chicago but stay black and die.

(Stunned silence. Everyone leaves but JOPLIN *and* CHAUVIN.)

JOPLIN

You were too young to die.

CHAUVIN

Twenty-six and tired.

JOPLIN

The sportin' house life. I warned you.

CHAUVIN

And look at you, Joplin. Look at you now. Brain turnin' to cotton. Anyway, I didn't die of the sportin' house life. Never went upstairs too much myself. Never got poxed like you. Never too much afflicted with love. I stayed in the parlor. Played and drank. Drank some. Played some. Drank. Played. Keys on strings. Then something went wrong along my nerves. Got the shakes and tremors. Got the galloping screaming meemies. Lost the feel in my fingers. Couldn't find the keys no more. Could still hear the notes. But couldn't find the keys.

(Pause)

CHAUVIN

Couldn't move my hands to play. But I could still hear melodies. Counterpoints. I could feel the bass line rubbing my heart.

*(*CHAUVIN *lets out a long anguished cry. A moment of silence follows. He smiles.)*

CHAUVIN

Couldn't do that either. Paralyzed. Couldn't talk, couldn't cry. Inside my useless body I still lived. And

no one knew. No one knew. Far away. Trapped. Like I
was trapped in a tunnel. Buried alive in my own body.

                    JOPLIN
That's a terrible way to die. Without music. Without
hope.

                    CHAUVIN
Terrible.

(He shrugs. Pause.)

                    JOPLIN
You remember *The Heliotrope Bouquet*?

                    CHAUVIN
I do, do you?

                    JOPLIN
Of course. Every day of my life. John Stark—

                    CHAUVIN
Your white man—

                    JOPLIN
My publisher. Said it was sublime. The audible poetry
of motion. His exact words.

                    CHAUVIN
The only piece of music mine was ever written down.
I ought to thank you.

                    JOPLIN
You're welcome.

                    CHAUVIN
I never got my money.

                    JOPLIN
I didn't take it. John Stark said you couldn't be found.

CHAUVIN

I could have used that money, Joplin.

JOPLIN

Couldn't be found, no. John Stark said you could not be found.

(JOHN STARK *appears.*)

STARK

Looked all over Chicago for you, Chauvin. The natural genius of piano ragtime.

CHAUVIN

Shoulda looked under my rock, Mr. Stark.

STARK

Could not be found. Asked high and low. Louis Chauvin, you know him? Ragtime natural genius and co-author with the King of Ragtime, i.e., Scott Joplin, *The Heliotrope Bouquet.* A slow drag two-step. A piece of music which is the audible poetry of motion.

CHAUVIN

What does that mean, Mr. Stark?

STARK

Pure motion, pure energy, pure delight. Blake said, energy is delight. Delight is energy. Something like that. Something along those lines.

JOPLIN

Thank you.

STARK

Pure energy, pure delight.

CHAUVIN

I guess I can rest easy, now.

STARK

Yes, indeed, you'll be remembered.

JOPLIN

If time is kind. If our children live, we'll all be remembered.

STARK

We'll be remembered. We'll be remembered as if we were gods.

CHAUVIN

If wishes were horses. If beggars could choose. If the river was whiskey, and I was a diving duck.

STARK

Yes, indeed, Chauvin. If you live, your time will come.

CHAUVIN

And if I don't?

STARK

You'll be remembered.

JOPLIN

Thanks to Mr. Stark.

CHAUVIN

Thanks to you, Joplin.

(CHAUVIN *disappears.*)

STARK

P'raps he's sore I held his money all these years till I heard he passed away.

JOPLIN

Always was a broody man.

STARK

Held it in trust. Accumulated interest, compounded
annual. Sorry I never could find him. And while I'm at
it, while I'm here, as long as I'm in the neighborhood,
let me publish your opera.

JOPLIN

Treemonisha.

STARK

Treemonisha.

(He picks up the manuscript.)

STARK

This it here?

JOPLIN

Yes Sir, Mr. Stark.

STARK

We'll cause a sensation. More than this single copy,
I hope.

JOPLIN

Yes, Sir.

STARK

Then I'll take this with me.

JOPLIN

I'm not done.

STARK

Doesn't matter.

JOPLIN

Let me finish.

STARK

Doesn't matter. Send the rest. What I'll do for you, Scott
Joplin. Acclaim, success, and freedom from care. The
crowned heads of Europe meet the King of Ragtime.
The toast of La Scala. The Great Gilt Houses. A Chopin
Joplin double bill. They'll be rocking on their
foundations with applause. Sipping champagne from
the chandeliers. A serious place in serious music
history. The adoration of multitudes. The respect of
critics. A paragraph in the encyclopaedia. Just what you
deserve, at last. Nothing less. You'll be remembered.

(STARK *hands the manuscript back to* JOPLIN.)

STARK

When you finish. On second thought.

JOPLIN

Aren't you gonna—take it now. Please, Mr. Stark.

STARK

Thought I'd deserted you. Scott Joplin. Man I crowned
King of Ragtime. Man I made immortal. Telling people
I turned my back.

JOPLIN

Never said that.

STARK

People exaggerate.

JOPLIN

Yes, they do.

STARK

I never cheated you. I always paid you your royalty.
I always paid you your due. I did my best.

JOPLIN

I know that, Mr. Stark. Won't you take this?

(He tries to give the manuscript back to STARK, *who demurs.)*

STARK

When you're done. Better hurry and finish. Ain't got
much time.

JOPLIN

Who?

STARK

Time's running out. Never enough. Never as much as
a person thinks. Hurrying to the end. Everybody wants
to go to heaven, but nobody wants to die.

JOPLIN

Where did you hear that, Mr. Stark?

*(*STARK *starts to fade away.)*

STARK

Hope you have more than one. More than one copy of
that work. Of *Treemonisha*. Remember the one you lost.
The ragtime opera you lost.

JOPLIN

The Guest of Honor.

STARK

Lost in the mail, wasn't it? Destroyed in a rooming
house fire? Left in a bar on a drunken binge? Purloined
from the Library of Congress? Something like that.
Something along those lines. Hope you have more
than one. More than one copy of that work. That
Treemonisha. Man can't stand to lose two life's works
in one lifetime.

JOPLIN

That was in St. Louis. With Belle, Sir. When the baby
died.

(STARK *is gone, and* BELLE *has appeared behind* JOPLIN.
She is holding a bundle.)

BELLE

Oh, Joplin.

JOPLIN

Belle. I'm so sorry.

BELLE

Coughed herself right out of this world and into the
next. Poor creature. Tiny thing. Never knew a word.

JOPLIN

I'm so sorry. If I could find my work. If I could just find
my work.

BELLE

What work? What are you talking about?

JOPLIN

The Guest of Honor. My opera. My ragtime opera.
Mislaid. Misplaced. Where's it gone? Help me find it.
If I could find that work, if I could just find that work,
I could bring our baby back.

BELLE

Don't talk foolish.

JOPLIN

We could start over.

BELLE

I can't stay here.

JOPLIN

We'll go away to Chicago.

BELLE

You'll go.

(JOPLIN *grabs her.*)

JOPLIN

Don't go. Don't go. Don't go.

BELLE

I'm sore, Joplin. A walking bruise. A lame dog and
a broken wheel. Singing never saved a soul. Singing
never brought nobody back. Once you're dead you're
done. I'm done, Joplin. Dead on my feet. I got no love
for you or any man. Love died with my baby.

JOPLIN

Don't go. Don't go. Don't go.

(*He shakes her. She drops the bundle and screams.*)

BELLE

Joplin.

(*The bundle hits the floor and scatters; plums roll across the
floor.*)

(*The lights change.* BELLE *becomes* LOTTIE, *and stands before*
JOPLIN.)

LOTTIE

Joplin. Look what you made me do.

(*She scurries about and picks up plums.*)

LOTTIE

They were perfect. And now they're bruised. Ruined.
Just like life. Like getting old. You make me tired.
Old man, you called me Belle again. Damn you.

JOPLIN

Sorry.

LOTTIE

Now sit.

JOPLIN

So sorry, Lottie. So sorry.

(He sits at the piano. LOTTIE puts the plums in a bowl and sets them before him. SPICE enters with coffee.)

JOPLIN

Who's that?

SPICE

Spice, Sir.

LOTTIE

Joplin. It's Spice. She's been here three months. You know who she is. Now hush.

(SPICE sets down the tray.)

SPICE

Chicory coffee, Mr. Joplin, and hot milk.

JOPLIN

A little lick of New Orleans. Thank you, girl.

(SPICE turns to go.)

JOPLIN

Girl?

SPICE

Yes, Sir.

JOPLIN

You're not one of them fancy ladies?

SPICE

Sir?

JOPLIN

One of those filles des joi we got upstairs?

LOTTIE

Oh, Joplin.

SPICE

No, Sir. I help Mrs. Joplin. Chores and such.

LOTTIE

That's enough.

JOPLIN

All right.

LOTTIE

Run along.

(SPICE *approaches* JOPLIN *shyly.*)

SPICE

Sir, my mama said. I said I was working for you.
I told her, she said. She said you were famous.

JOPLIN

Told you that.

SPICE

Yes, Sir.

JOPLIN

I was famous long ago, child. When I was your age.
When your mama was your age. And you were only
one of a million things that might have happened.
(Pause) You could be my daughter. She'd be about your
age. Prob'ly doing what you're doing. Fetch and serve.

Scrub, cook, work for other folks. Most folks never taste
what I have tasted.

SPICE

Sir. Play me? My mama said I should ask you. Could
you play me something? Mr. Joplin? Please, Sir, please?

JOPLIN

Can't play no more.

SPICE

My mama said I should ask you.

*(He waits. He spreads his hands several times over the
keyboard, testing. He waits. Nothing comes. His hands hover
over the keys. Waiting. Nothing comes. A long pause, poised
over the keyboard.)*

(He gives up. Sags.)

JOPLIN

Sorry, girl, can't play no more. Can't play a lick. Too
old, too tired, too sick. Too sore. Been around the world
and back. I was famous long ago. Most folks never taste
what I have tasted. Now people forgot about me like
I never been born. Gone, gone, gone. All that's gone.
Done.

LOTTIE

Shoo now, Spice. Take coffee upstairs. The girls will be
wanting some.

(SPICE scurries off. JOPLIN mutters.)

JOPLIN

Whores in my house. Can't nothing good come of
keeping whores.

current check-outs summary for GRET ANDE
Mon Jul 09 19:28:26 CDT 2012

BARCODE: R0102219676
TITLE: Scott Joplin : a life in ragtime
DUE DATE: Jul 23 2012

BARCODE: 33477000313822
TITLE: Treemonisha : vocal score / Scott
DUE DATE: Jul 23 2012

BARCODE: R0120969732
TITLE: The heliotrope bouquet by Scott J
DUE DATE: Jul 23 2012

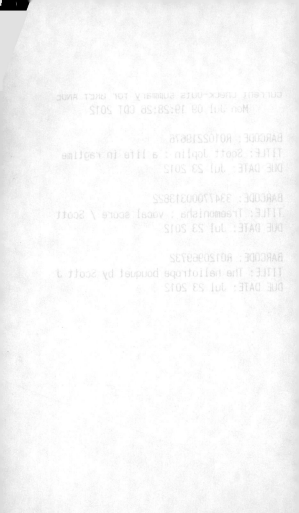

LOTTIE

How are we to live? Tell me that. Now drink your coffee and take a rest.

(She starts to go. JOPLIN *notices the electric Christmas tree on the piano.)*

JOPLIN

What's that doing here?

LOTTIE

Oh, Joplin. It's Christmas Eve.

JOPLIN

Is it? I forgot.

LOTTIE

You'd forget your head, if you could. If it weren't screwed on.

JOPLIN

Thought maybe I was back in St. Louis. Before I knew you. Did I ever tell you about the Rosebud Cafe? And the cutting contest? Chauvin won.

LOTTIE

Did you ever not? Just every Christmas Eve.

JOPLIN

That tree reminds me—

LOTTIE

That's why we got it—

JOPLIN/LOTTIE

Of the Rosebud Cafe.

(She goes.)

JOPLIN

Oh, Belle. You disappeared. Never a word of you again.
Wondering where you are. Wondering where you are,
all these years. Miss you every day. Every day of my
life. Wondering where you are.

(CHAUVIN *appears behind him.* JOPLIN *senses his presence.*
Turns and sees CHAUVIN, *who comes over to the piano.*
JOPLIN, *watching* CHAUVIN, *puts his hands on the piano*
and begins to play—slowly at first, then, gradually, with
transformed youthful energy—a beautiful rag. As JOPLIN
plays, with CHAUVIN *watching, the lights fade to black.*
They come up on:)

Part Two

(CHAUVIN's *Rock*)

(*Chicago, 1906. The Sportin' Life, an opium den.*
CHAUVIN *is smoking an opium pipe.)*

CHAUVIN

The Sportin' Life.

(*Music plays. Two couples, a man and a woman, and*
a woman and a woman, dance a slow, sensual, languid,
liquid tango.)

CHAUVIN

The floor is satin
The ceiling's stars
The air is flashy with ribbons and pearls
Come on in
It's always Christmas in an opium den
This subtle smoke
Is the breath of God
Taste it
Come on in taste it
This subtle smoke
Is the breath of God

Taste it
Come on in taste it
This subtle smoke
The breath of God

(JOPLIN *appears.*)

JOPLIN

The Sportin' Life.

CHAUVIN

Yes, yes, yes, The Sportin' Life. That's the very name of
this here place. The Sportin' Life.

JOPLIN

The one I warned you about. How can you stand it?

CHAUVIN

What a question. I can't stand it nowhere else. I'm raw.
Like a baby got no skin. And daylight hurts my eyes.
This place is soft. This place is easy. This place is full
of places I have never been. Full of all kind of strange
and wonderful. I float to China here and talk to dead
Emperors. I been to Africa and back, to Ashanti and
Ghana, Dahomey and Timbuktu. I been over to Peru
to warn the Incas 'bout Pizarro. Thought he was their
long lost white brother. Long lost white brother? I said,
watch your neck, and save us all a trip to the New
World.

JOPLIN

Did they listen?

CHAUVIN

Nah. Fools. These walls are sweaty with dreaming. I
lick these walls and I dream other folks' dreams. I hear
bells and chimes from heaven. Whistles and horns from
hell. Angels and ancestors. And notes on the piano that
are not there. That are not even there. This place is soft

and easy and I can play here. And the rags flow
through my fingers. And I don't have no need to
write them down. I smoke my smoke, and I remember
everything. And forget everything, too. Remember it
all, and forget about it all, in the same breath.

JOPLIN

Ain't real. Ain't real. Won't last. Pour sunshine on this
place, it'd curl up and die.

CHAUVIN

Don't tell me what's real. Ain't for you to say. Mr.
Joplin. Mr. Cautious Joplin. Always with one eye
on the future.

JOPLIN

I had a notion I could make my life shine.

CHAUVIN

Funny how things turn out.

JOPLIN

But I did. I took my gift and opened it.

CHAUVIN

For a time, maybe. But nothing lasts forever—wouldn't
you say?

JOPLIN

Maybe. Some things last.

CHAUVIN

Last as long as a man can stay awake. Then they're
gone. Life's a dream they say. An opium dream.
What brings you here?

JOPLIN

Looking for you.

CHAUVIN

Why on earth?

JOPLIN

Know we got something to do together. Got to write
together. Something fine. Want to get you published.
Get you down on paper. So people will remember.
So you will be remembered. Some things last.

CHAUVIN

Remembered for my association with the King of
Ragtime?

JOPLIN

Remembered for yourself. Your music.

CHAUVIN

In amongst the dope fiends, the King of Ragtime.
What brings you here?

JOPLIN

Looking for you. I thought we might write something
together. What's the matter? Can't you hear me through
your subtle smoke?

CHAUVIN

Somebody told me, came running in here one day,
waving a piece of music and saying this guy's the
King of Rag, the King of Rag*time*. Not you, not Louis
Chauvin, who can't even read his own name, and I said
do tell, who would that be, and he said, this here fella
Joplin. And I looked up and there you were, large as
life and twice as ugly. *Maple Leaf Rag.*

JOPLIN

Grieves me you don't like it.

CHAUVIN

But I do. Oh yes I do. My favorite. What brings you
here?

JOPLIN

My daughter died. My wife left me.

CHAUVIN

Why didn't you say so? Life's a sorry poxy clapped-up
bitch and a fading faulty memory. Come on in. This
place here is as good a place as any to hide from her.
The old whore. Life, I mean.

JOPLIN

The feeling's on me. Stirring. Had the fever. Woke up in
the middle of the night, staring at the ceiling. Had the
fever urge to work. Start over. Start new. Make music.
We'll write. I'll get what we do published.

CHAUVIN

Like your famous. Like your world famous song,
Maple Leaf Rag.

JOPLIN

That's right. John Stark will pay us. Our creation.

CHAUVIN

Mr. Stark. Your white man.

JOPLIN

My publisher. That's the future, Chauvin. Got to have
one eye on the future. Got to think about it before it
happens.

CHAUVIN

Far as I'm concerned, the day after tomorrow might as
well be springtime on the moon.

(Pause. JOPLIN*'s stymied.* CHAUVIN *considers. Then:)*

CHAUVIN

I'm ready. Got a piece of music been rattling in my
brain for days now like a lonely candy in a quart jar.
Won't leave me alone at night.

(JOPLIN *looks. The denizens of the opium den are slumbering
on the piano.*)

JOPLIN

We need the piano.

CHAUVIN

They're sleeping on the piano.

(CHAUVIN *gestures, and the electric Christmas tree lights
up.*)

JOPLIN

Is it Christmas?

CHAUVIN

It's always Christmas in an opium den. Merry
Christmas, Joplin. Want to hear my latest composition?
Christmas In An Opium Den Rag?

JOPLIN

I can't work here.

CHAUVIN

This is where I am. This is where I live. You staying and
playing, or you praying and promenading?

(JOPLIN *considers. Looks at the denizens.*)

JOPLIN

Let's play. But just us alone.

CHAUVIN

I can make them go away. It's my dream, not yours.
My fever dream, my very own. You're not even here.

JOPLIN
I'm dreaming you. I'm dreaming you dreaming.

CHAUVIN
Are you sure? Maybe I'm dreaming you dreaming me
dreaming.

JOPLIN
That's way too subtle for me.

CHAUVIN
We're dreaming each other dreaming each other.

JOPLIN
Then dream you make them go away.

CHAUVIN
All right. You say so. You're my guest. You're my
dream.

(CHAUVIN *gestures to the denizens.*)

CHAUVIN
Depart. Vanish. Perambulate. Leave this dream.
Go console yourselves elsewhere. Dansez d'ici.

(*He waves his hands. An orchestral dance plays. The
denizens couple up, do a dreamy, macabre opium dance
and disappear, leaving* JOPLIN *and* CHAUVIN *alone.*)

CHAUVIN
Never heard a rag like that, did you, Mr. King of the
Ragtime Piano? *Christmas In An Opium Den Rag.*

JOPLIN
I always said you were the best. Everybody knew that.
Wasn't me who crowned me King.

CHAUVIN
People forgot about me. Like I never been born.

JOPLIN

Let's make some music. Can you, are you able?

CHAUVIN

I'm fine. Fresh as the day my momma first laid eyes on
me. Let's do it. Let's create.

(CHAUVIN *goes to the piano, sits. Silence. He listens.
Then he plays the middle section of* The Heliotrope
Bouquet.)

CHAUVIN

I hear the heliotrope. A heliotrope bouquet. Blossoms
now in my brain. Hear it? Hear the flower open? Hear it
root? Hear the way it buds and blossoms, dying for the
light. Listen.

(JOPLIN *listens as* CHAUVIN *plays. Then:*)

JOPLIN

I hear it.

(CHAUVIN *plays again.*)

CHAUVIN

Hear the way it's worn? Heliotrope flower, pinned
in a young girl's curly black hair. All down her back.
Bunches cut in bundles tossed down on a maple table.
Stuck in a blue glass pitcher. Hear those flowers draw
water as long as they can—sucking at life like a
drowning man. Hear how the heliotrope bouquet wilts
and dries, swoons and withers, curls up and blackens
and dies. Hear how fast its beauty fades away?

(*He finishes. Turns to* JOPLIN.)

CHAUVIN

I feel better now. That ribbon's been winding through
my dreams for days. Keeping me awake at night. That's

my part. You do the rest. I'm not so good with endings.
You're the man to tell me how it winds up.

(CHAUVIN *gets up*. JOPLIN *takes his place at the piano*.)

JOPLIN

You don't leave me much.

(He begins to play.)

JOPLIN

Water and dirt, color, sap and pollen. Perfume. And a
ripple of wind. Fields of heliotrope. Purple and white.
The reappearance of spring. Come round again.

(He plays. He stops.)

CHAUVIN

That's a start. Now what comes after, what follows?
State your intention. Your honor, Sir, Mr. King of
Ragtime Highness.

(JOPLIN *plays*.)

JOPLIN

Midsummer. Solstice. Full moon blossoms. Grows fat
and full. Swells. Peaks. Pops. Comes. Gushes forth,
life's sweet honey. Wax and wane. Wax and wane.
Consummation. Culmination. Climax. Ripeness.
And after ripeness, after ripeness—sweet resolution.

(He plays. He stops. They both consider.)

CHAUVIN

Sweet resolution. That's the difference between music
and life.

(JOPLIN *plays the entire* Heliotrope Bouquet. CHAUVIN
does a dreamy dance. JOPLIN *finishes playing. Silence.*
The sound of one person applauding. JOHN STARK *appears.*)

STARK

The audible poetry of motion. Pure energy, pure
delight. The only written remnant of the legendary
Louis Chauvin left to the ages. The greatest ragtime
player ever, who otherwise would have vanished from
memory.

JOPLIN

From human memory.

STARK

From human memory. Still to be heard in the ether and
the House of God.

JOPLIN

And in my head till my dying day.

STARK

Indeed. The Legendary Louis Chauvin, preserved here
in my publication, *The Heliotrope Bouquet* by Scott Joplin
and Louis Chauvin. This moment between two creative
titans, this crossing of comets, this spark, this gossamer
explosion, this fragile, wet, shimmering creation, this
newborn dragonfly, this exquisite cry of an exotic bird
hunted to extinction for its brilliant plumage—this
sheer ephemera. I saved it. Preserved for posterity.
Lightning positively captured in a bottle. The audible
poetry of motion. Pure energy, pure delight. The only
written remnant of Louis Chauvin. The legendary Louis
Chauvin.

CHAUVIN

Sweet resolution. That's the difference between music
and this life. I find my consolation in the piano and the
pipe. Music's in the smoke, in the heliotrope.

JOPLIN

Still to be heard in the ether and the House of God.
Chauvin's piano ringing ragtime in the House of God.

(BELLE *appears.*)

BELLE

Wondering where you are.

JOPLIN

Belle.

BELLE

If the river were whisky. If wishes were horses. If we
didn't have to die. If only life was sweet enough to
want to live forever.

CHAUVIN

The House of God. Is that a Sportin' House?

JOPLIN

You're not as bitter as you pretend to be.

CHAUVIN

How would you know?

BELLE

Hear the way it's worn. Heliotrope flower pinned in a
young girl's hair. Curly black hair all down her back.
Before she knows what's coming. Before her life has
passed her by.

(JOPLIN *goes to* BELLE.)

JOPLIN

I gave it up early. Wanted to make my life shine.
And I did. I opened my gift.

BELLE

Oh you did, yes you did, Joplin.

(CHAUVIN *turns to* STARK.)

CHAUVIN
You never paid me a penny.

STARK
I didn't cheat you, Chauvin.

CHAUVIN
You never paid me my money.

STARK
I rescued you. I saved your work. Now people not yet
born can trace your thoughts, follow the flight of your
fingers across the keys, feel how your heart beat, how
your breath went in and out as you made that song.
I brought you back from the brink of oblivion.

CHAUVIN
You should have looked under my rock, Mr. Stark.

(CHAUVIN *glances at* BELLE, *then* JOPLIN. *They stop
dancing.*)

CHAUVIN
Don't believe in fate. Don't believe in God. Just luck.
Bad luck, good luck. Bad luck, mostly, for most folks,
most of the time. I was lucky for a little while. Then I
wasn't.

STARK
The audible poetry of motion.

CHAUVIN
I'll never know. What's a published piece to me?
Can't read.

JOPLIN
You'll die too young.

CHAUVIN

You'll live too long. Funny how things turn out. You're
the one who'll fade away. Brain turnin' to cotton. Done
in by the sportin' life. The one you always warned me
about.

JOPLIN

I stopped going upstairs early. Wanted to make my life
shine. And I did. One mistake. The past came back and
ripped me up, ripped me open, like a rabid dog. Tore
me up bad. Unforgiving.

CHAUVIN

Funny how things turn out. I ain't gonna dream about
you any more, Joplin. *(To* STARK*)* Brought me back from
oblivion, did you?

STARK

Did my best.

CHAUVIN

Wasn't enough. Whatever you did, wasn't enough.
I died like a dog and lived worse. You should have
looked here, under my rock. You owe me, Mr. Stark.
I ain't gonna dream about you no more, neither.

(CHAUVIN disappears. STARK *starts to fade off, as the light
changes.)*

STARK

So bitter. To be so sour, even beyond the grave.
I did what I could. I treated you right.

JOPLIN

Never said you didn't.

STARK

People exaggerate.

JOPLIN

Yes, they do. My new opera—it's almost finished—

(JOPLIN *picks up the manuscript.*)

STARK

What's the hurry? Let me know when you're done.
Drop me a line, Joplin. Take good care.

JOPLIN

Please, Mr. Stark. Why won't you take this?

(*The lights are fading back to Harlem, 1917.* JOPLIN *holds out the manuscript. He listens to* STARK's *voice fading away.*)

STARK

You'll get the respect that's due you at last. A serious
place in serious music history. The adulation of
multitudes. The crowned heads of Europe. A Joplin
Chopin double bill. A paragraph in the encyclopaedia.
An obituary in *The New York Times*. When you're
finished. When you're done. Take your time. Let me
know.

(STARK *fades away completely.* JOPLIN *is left clutching his opera score.* LOTTIE *appproaches. He turns and looks at her. It takes him a moment to recognize her.*)

JOPLIN

Belle.

LOTTIE

Oh, Joplin. No, not Belle.

JOPLIN

She was here.

LOTTIE

This is Lottie. The second one. The one saved your
sorry life, remember?

JOPLIN

Oh, Lottie, yes. Yes, my wife. My darling. Good soul.

LOTTIE

Thank you.

JOPLIN

Belle was here.

LOTTIE

Only in your dreams.

JOPLIN

And Chauvin.

LOTTIE

What did he want?

JOPLIN

Tell me I was right. Some things last. He heard what I said. He took it to heart. We wrote *The Heliotrope Bouquet* together.

LOTTIE

Oh, Joplin. That's my favorite. *The Heliotrope.*

JOPLIN

I know. He did the first part. I did the last.

LOTTIE

A sweet song. Sweet as twilight. Sweet as a Sea Island breeze. Sweet as my sweet youth, and my lost body.

JOPLIN

Some things last.

(He stands motionless, lost in reverie. She leads him to the piano, and he sits. Then:)

JOPLIN

Mr. Stark was here, too.

LOTTIE

Yes?

JOPLIN

Yes. He's going to publish my opera.

LOTTIE

Treemonisha.

JOPLIN

My masterpiece. Soon as I finish. Mr. Stark will publish
it. I'll be redeemed. My little baby, I'll bring her back.

LOTTIE

Oh, Joplin. Mr. Stark turned his back on you years ago.

JOPLIN

I remember.

LOTTIE

Said he wouldn't publish that opera. Said no one would
ever do that piece.

JOPLIN

Times were hard. The bloom was off the ragtime rose.

LOTTIE

Oh, Joplin. You always defended him.

JOPLIN

He always paid me my royalty. He always paid me my
due. *(Pause)* Ragtime's gone. Ragtime's over. Ragtime's
done. *(Pause)* I just have to finish. You'll see. I just have
to finish. Still time. While there's still time.

(SPICE enters, with a wreath, ribbons, Christmas decorations.)

JOPLIN

Who's that?

SPICE

Spice, Sir.

LOTTIE

Oh, Joplin, you know who she is.

JOPLIN

Come here, child.

(SPICE *goes to* JOPLIN. *He takes her hand.*)

JOPLIN

Pretty child. Where you been?

SPICE

Upstairs.

JOPLIN

I mean all these years.

SPICE

Sir?

JOPLIN

I been worried about you. Your mama told me you
were dead.

(LOTTIE *becomes* BELLE. *[To* JOPLIN, *not to* SPICE,
of course.])

BELLE

She was dead, Joplin. Cold as snow, and all her color
gone. But I found your score.

JOPLIN

The Guest of Honor?

BELLE

The one you lost.

SPICE

Sir?

BELLE

Brought it to Mr. Stark, which he published to great
acclaim. And that's what brought our baby back to life.
The sound of your songs sung reached heaven, and
touched God's heart, and breathed breath back into our
baby.

JOPLIN

I knew that would happen. I knew if I could find that
lost score, my lost music....

BELLE

And now she's here. Same age she'd be as if she lived.
A young woman. A grown woman. Pretty girl.

JOPLIN

I knew there was music to wake the dead.

(JOPLIN *holds her hand more tightly. She's frightened.*)

SPICE

Please, Mr. Joplin, Sir.

(LOTTIE *moves to* JOPLIN *and* SPICE.)

LOTTIE

Stop, now. You're scaring the poor child.

JOPLIN

No, I'm just so glad to see her after all this time.
(*To* SPICE) You been a good girl?

SPICE

I do my best, Sir.

LOTTIE
He's having a spell, child. Don't pay him no mind.

JOPLIN
Pretty child.

(LOTTIE *disengages* SPICE'*s hand from* JOPLIN'*s.*)

LOTTIE
Run along now. The upstairs parlor needs a dust.

SPICE
Yes, Ma'am.

(*She leaves.*)

JOPLIN
Such a pretty girl. Our daughter's beautiful.

LOTTIE
That's Spice, the serving girl. Oh, what's the use?
Life's a sorry bitch and a fading memory.

JOPLIN
Belle.

(*He turns to where* BELLE *was last standing. She's gone.*)

LOTTIE
Was she here again?

JOPLIN
Yes.

LOTTIE
Ghosts come and go. That's the advantage of being a
ghost. You can do as you damn well please.

JOPLIN
I wrote that song in Chicago.

LOTTIE

I know.

JOPLIN

Heliotrope. With Chauvin. Tracked him down to an
opium den. He died young.

LOTTIE

The good die young.

JOPLIN

He wasn't good.

LOTTIE

He was a good piano player.

JOPLIN

Yes, indeed. Your favorite.

LOTTIE

Never heard him play.

JOPLIN

No, the song. *Heliotrope.*

LOTTIE

Always.

JOPLIN

Did I write that song before I knew you, or after?

LOTTIE

Doesn't matter.

JOPLIN

I wrote it for you, whether I knew it or not. Whether I
knew you or not.

LOTTIE

For me, or for Belle?

JOPLIN

For you, Lottie. Belle's dead. Belle's dead and gone. Done.

LOTTIE

Wish I could believe that.

JOPLIN

Long time gone. All these years. Wondering where, wondering where she is, where she went. Disappeared. Dear Lottie. My heart was broken before I knew you.

LOTTIE

Was it?

JOPLIN

Oh Lottie, yes.

LOTTIE

My heart was broken since I knew you, Joplin.

(She turns on the electric Christmas tree. It lights up; JOPLIN is delighted, like a child. He claps his hands.)

JOPLIN

All kind of strange and wonderful.

(LOTTIE leaves.)

JOPLIN

Still time. Still time. While there's still time.

(JOPLIN spreads out his score before him.)

JOPLIN

If I were with my love, I would live forever.

(He sits at the piano. Motionless. A new rag plays in the ether, all kind of strange and wonderful, unlike anything we've heard before.)

(Paralyzed, he listens as it plays, unable to write it down. The tricks, whores, and professors of the Sportin' House of his youth appear, and do a slow, elegant dance in the dying light. As they dance, the light eventually fades to twilight. Everyone disappears.)

(SPICE and BELLE appear in a light. JOPLIN sees them, draws himself up, revived, becomes young again, puts his hands on the piano, and begins to play The Heliotrope Bouquet. SPICE and BELLE disappear.)

(As JOPLIN plays, CHAUVIN appears, and approaches the piano. He leans on the piano and listens to JOPLIN play their composition. As the song finishes, the lights fade very slowly to black.)